American ANIMALS

BALD EAGLES

Meryl Magby

PowerKiDS press
New York

Published in 2012 by The Rosen Publishing Group, Inc.
29 East 21st Street, New York, NY 10010

First Edition

Editor: Amelie von Zumbusch
Book Design: Ashley Drago

Photo Credits: Cover Sylvain Cordier/Getty Images; pp. 4, 10, 16, 18–19 © www.iStockphoto.com/ Frank Leung; p. 5 James Brey/Getty Images; pp. 6, 7 (left, bottom), 8, 11 Shutterstock.com; p. 9 © www.iStockphoto.com/Brent Paull; pp. 12–13 Guy Crittenden/Getty Images; p. 14 © www.iStockphoto. com/Ken Canning; p. 15 © www.iStockphoto.com/John Henderson; p. 17 Klaus Nigge/Getty Images; p. 20 Loomis Dean/Time & Life Pictures/Getty Images; p. 21 Tom Brakefield/Stockbyte/Thinkstock; p. 22 Jupiterimages/Liquidlibrary/Thinkstock.

Library of Congress Cataloging-in-Publication Data

Magby, Meryl.
 Bald eagles / by Meryl Magby. — 1st ed.
     p. cm. — (American animals)
Includes index.
ISBN 978-1-4488-6180-4 (library binding) — ISBN 978-1-4488-6319-8 (pbk.) —
ISBN 978-1-4488-6320-4 (6-pack)
1. Bald eagle–Juvenile literature. I. Title.
QL696.F32M2575 2012
598.9'45—dc23

                                          2011023956

Manufactured in the United States of America

CPSIA Compliance Information: Batch #WW12PK: For Further Information contact Rosen Publishing, New York, New York at 1-800-237-9932

Contents

An American Symbol

Bald eagles are one of the best-known animals in North America. This is because they are the national **symbol** of the United States. Many people know what bald eagles look like. You can see their picture on the backs of dollar bills. However, there was a time when bald eagles almost died out.

Bald eagles are sea eagles. Sea eagles tend to live near the water and eat fish. Other sea eagles include Steller's sea eagles and African fish eagles.

Today, American bald eagle **populations** are growing. Bald eagles are one of two **species** of eagles found in the United States. The other species is the golden eagle. Golden eagles can be found in North America, Europe, Asia, and Africa. Bald eagles live only in North America.

Bald eagles are among North America's biggest birds.

Living Near Water

All bald eagles live near water. This eagle is soaring above the Pacific Ocean off the coast of Alaska.

Bald eagles can be found in every US state except for Hawaii. They live in parts of Canada and Mexico, too. Bald eagles most often live in forests near bodies of water, such as large lakes, rivers, reservoirs, swamps, and marshes. They also live along the coasts of the Atlantic Ocean and the Pacific Ocean.

Bald eagles that live in places with cold winters will fly to other areas when it gets too cold. This is because the bodies of water in these places freeze in the winter. Eagles cannot get to the fish they eat if the surface of the water is frozen.

A large number of eagles live in Alaska. The state is home to more than 30,000 bald eagles.

This bald eagle is in Nevada. Nevada is one of the places bald eagles from colder parts of North America spend the winter.

White, Yellow, and Brown

Bald eagles' feet have four toes. They have three toes in front and one in back.

Adult bald eagles have white heads and tails, light yellow eyes, and bright yellow beaks and feet. Their bodies are very dark brown. Their long beaks have hooked tips for tearing apart their food. They have sharp **talons** on each toe that are about 2 inches (5 cm) long.

Bald eagles are one of the largest **raptors**, or birds of prey, in North America. Their **wingspan**, or the distance between the tips of their wings, is about 6 to 8 feet (2–2.4 m). Adults generally weigh between 8 and 15 pounds (4–7 kg). Female eagles are slightly larger than males.

Bald eagles' bodies are most often about 3 feet (1 m) long.

Feathers and Flying

The bodies of bald eagles are covered with feathers. It is easy to tell adult bald eagles and young bald eagles apart. This is because their feathers, or **plumage**, are different colors. Adult eagles have white heads and tails. Young eagles are mostly

Another way to spot a bald eagle is to look at the feathers at the tips of its wings. They are spaced apart widely.

brown with spots of white and cream on their undersides. They look like this until they are about four or five years old.

Young bald eagles are often mistaken for golden eagles or turkey vultures. You can tell a bald eagle apart from these other birds because it flies with its wings straight out.

Bald Eagle Facts

1. In the wild, bald eagles may live for between 20 and 30 years. However, there have been bald eagles in **captivity** that have lived to be about 50 years old.

2. The bald eagle's scientific name is *Haliaeetus leucocephalus.* It means "sea eagle with white head."

3. Alaska is the state with the biggest bald eagle population. It has more eagles than the rest of the country put together.

4. Bald eagles have very good eyesight. In fact, they can see five to six times better than people can.

5. The largest population of bald eagles in the Midwest lives along the Mississippi River. Between 2,500 and 4,000 bald eagles spend the winter there each year.

6. At night, bald eagles **roost** together. They choose tall trees that keep them safe from wind and rain for roosting.

7. Each bald eagle has about 7,000 feathers on its body.

8. Bald eagles can fly at speeds of between 36 and 44 miles per hour (58–71 km/h).

9. The bald eagle was picked as the emblem of the United States in 1782. An emblem is an official symbol.

Hunting for Food

Bald eagles eat mostly fish. However, they will eat waterfowl, small mammals, or dead animals if they cannot catch any fish. They also steal food caught by other birds, such as other raptors or gulls. However, bald eagles cannot carry prey that weighs more than 4 pounds (2 kg).

Bald eagles often grab fish right out of the water.

Bald eagles hunt for food during the day. They often perch on tree branches near the edge of the water to watch for fish. Then, they swoop down into the water to catch the fish and carry it away. They kill their prey with their sharp talons and use their beaks to tear it apart.

This bald eagle is eating a fish. Depending on where they live, bald eagles eat different kinds of fish.

Mating and Nesting

Bald eagles most often pick their mates when they are four or five years old.

Bald eagles generally **mate** during the winter months. During this time, pairs of male and female eagles can be seen doing loops, cartwheels, and dives while flying in the air. This is called courtship behavior. Once a bald eagle finds its mate, the two eagles stay together for life.

Bald eagle nests are big! They tend to be about 5 feet (1.5 m) wide. Some can be as wide as 9 feet (3 m).

After they have mated, the pairs of eagles then work together to build their nests. Male eagles collect **materials** for the nests and females build them. The nests are often made from large sticks, small twigs, and grass or moss. Once a pair of eagles has built a nest, they come back to it each year and add more material to it.

Time to Hatch!

Most female bald eagles lay between one and three eggs each spring. The eggs are laid a few days apart. For the next 35 days or so, the male and female eagles take turns **incubating** the eggs. This means they sit on the eggs to keep them warm. Once the eggs hatch, both parents bring fish to feed the chicks.

Bald eagle chicks can eat as much as 2 pounds (1 kg) of fish each day.

About 10 to 12 weeks after they hatch, young eagles learn to fly. Over the summer, the young eagles learn how to catch food by watching adult eagles. By winter, their parents leave them and they must take care of themselves.

Keeping Eagles Safe

The plane shown here is spraying DDT on crops in California in 1947. At the time, people used DDT to kill insects. They did not understand the dangers of DDT.

By the 1960s, there were very few bald eagles left in the wild. Many eagles lost their homes when large areas of forest were cut down. Others were killed because people thought that bald eagles were killing their farm animals.

Bald eagles almost died out totally because of a **pesticide** called DDT.

DDT caused eagles to lay eggs that cracked before their chicks hatched.

DDT became illegal in the United States in 1972. In 1973, Congress passed the **Endangered** Species Act. This made it illegal to kill certain animals, including bald eagles. Soon, the population of bald eagles began to grow again.

Bald Eagles Today

Today, bald eagles are no longer considered an endangered species. Killing them is now illegal. People have worked to set aside land for bald eagles.

There are many places in the United States where you can see bald eagles. However, if you see a bald eagle, do not get too close! You may disturb its nest site. This can cause adult eagles to not take care of their eggs. Watching bald eagles from a distance helps make sure that they will be around for years to come!

Bald eagles are beautiful, powerful birds. We can all be happy that they are still around today!

Glossary

captivity (kap-TIH-vih-tee) A place where animals live, such as in a home, a zoo, or an aquarium, instead of living in the wild.

endangered (in-DAYN-jerd) In danger of no longer existing.

incubating (IN-kyoo-bay-ting) Keeping eggs warm.

mate (MAYT) To come together to make babies.

materials (muh-TEER-ee-ulz) The things something is made of.

pesticide (PES-tuh-syd) A poison used to kill pests.

plumage (PLOO-mij) The feathers of a bird.

populations (pop-yoo-LAY-shunz) Groups of animals or people living in the same place.

raptors (RAP-terz) Sharp-clawed birds that hunt other animals.

roost (ROOST) To go to the place where one rests or sleeps.

species (SPEE-sheez) One kind of living thing. All people are one species.

symbol (SIM-bul) An object or a picture that stands for something else.

talons (TA-lunz) The strong, sharp-clawed feet of a bird that eats animals.

wingspan (WING-span) The distance from wing tip to wing tip when a bird's wings are stretched out.

Index

E

eggs, 18, 21–22
Endangered Species
Act, 21
Europe, 5

F

forest(s), 6, 20

L

lakes, 6

P

people, 4, 13,
20, 22
pesticide, 20
plumage, 10
population(s), 5,
13, 21

R

raptors, 9, 14
reservoirs, 6
river(s), 6, 13

S

species, 5, 22
state, 6, 13
swamps, 6
symbol, 4, 13

T

talons, 8, 15

W

wingspan, 9

Web Sites

Due to the changing nature of Internet links, PowerKids Press
has developed an online list of Web sites related to the subject
of this book. This site is updated regularly. Please use this link to
access the list:
www.powerkidslinks.com/aman/eagle/